WHO AM I?

JOURNAL
FOR DISCOVERING
PERSONAL WORTH

Great
GROUPS
DISCOVERY SERIES

ANNE DINNAN
LAUREL EDISON
KELLY D. PEAVEY

David C. Cook Publishing Co.
Elgin, Illinois/Paris, Ontario

While this journal can stand on its own, it is a companion to the *Who Am I? Leader's Guide* in the Great Groups Discovery Series. This series is written specifically for use in home Bible studies for older teens and young adults, both seekers and Christians. Participants may use these journals to help prepare for their small group study, or simply in their private quest for answers to life's ultimate questions.

GREAT GROUPS
Discovery Series
Who Am I? Journal
© 1994 David C. Cook Publishing Co.

Unless otherwise noted, Scripture quotations are from the Holy Bible, New International Version (NIV), © 1973, 1978, 1984 by International Bible Society. Used by permission of Zondervan Bible Publishers.
"ME I AM," poem on page 52, from *The Random House Book of Poetry for Children*, by Jack Prelutsky © 1983 by Jack Prelutsky. Reprinted by permission of Random House, Inc.
Unless otherwise noted, marginal quotes concerning Scripture or Christianity are from
Evidence that Demands a Verdict Vol. 1 by Josh McDowell, © 1972 by Campus Crusade for Christ.
Published by David C. Cook Publishing Co.
850 North Grove Avenue, Elgin, Illinois 60120
Cable address: DCCOOK
Series editor: Anne E. Dinnan. Contributors: Anne E. Dinnan, Laurel Edison, Kelly D. Peavey.
Designer: Jeff Sharpton, PAZ Design Group. Cover illustrator: Ken Cuffe.
Inside illustrator: Jim Carson.
Printed in U.S.A. ISBN: 0-7814-5134-5

WHO AM I?

The Private Devotional Journal of

_____

_____

TABLE OF Contents

Who Am I?

Introduction

The Bible is an ancient book. Why should we trust what it says? Well, for one thing, it never sugar-coats the truth. And for another thing, it is an ancient book. It hasn't changed for thousands of years, yet it's still as relevant today as it was when it was being written. This journal contains tid-bits of information about the Bible to show its credibility historically as well as its transcendent nature.

We invite you to come and check it out. This series does not pretend to answer all your questions. It simply invites you to approach the Bible as a potential source for answers. If there is a God, and if He is both personal and good, He is perfectly capable of speaking for Himself. That's what these studies are designed to let Him do.

Ways to Do This Journal

This is your personal journal. How much you benefit from journaling is up to you. Our hope is that you will discover more about who you are by writing in this journal at least once a week. May you discover your true significance as a child of God through your participation in these exercises.

This journal was written to go along with the small group Bible studies in the *Who Am I? Leader's Guide*. If you are using this with a small group, the questions, activities, and Scripture passages will help prepare you for the weekly study. However, you can also use this just as it is, all by itself.

There's a "Daily Markings" section in which you can record your thoughts about significant events of each day of the week. Then, each weekly section offers thought-provoking tidbits, questions, and Scripture study to help you journal in a more directed way. There are also some pages to record prayer requests and praises for you or your group.

May we suggest one thing? Even if you are not doing this as part of a group, will you find one person to share your thoughts with as you go through this journal? You are not alone!

Do I Matter?

Exploring My Significance

by Anne Dinnan

Who am I? Where did I come from? Why am I here? These are the questions that nag at every thinking human being. Science gives us some answers: Where did you come from? Well, it's like this. Your mother and your father. . . . But that's not really the question is it? Maybe you need to know if you were wanted by your mother and father. And if the answer is no, then what? Do you matter to anyone? Is there any point to existence at all? If we are simply the highest form that has evolved from the primordial slime, why do we suffer so much asking these pointless questions? Why can't we just be like the fish in the sea or the birds in the air? Somehow we want more.

The Bible offers answers to these ultimate questions, especially the one about mattering to someone. It says you matter to God even if you don't think you matter to any other human being on the face of the earth. And that answer makes a difference. In the coming weeks you will explore the Bible's answers for yourself. In this journal you can keep a record of your honest thoughts about those answers. Do you believe them? Do they satisfy?

Anne Dinnan, series editor, is leaving her comfortable position as a youth editor at David C. Cook and branching out in a new direction. She is completing M.A. studies at Wheaton Graduate School, preparing for missionary service. A former English major (Nyack College, N. Y.), Anne loves to read and discuss just about anything. Anne is big on cooperative ministry and is involved in a movement called Concerts of Prayer that seeks to bring Christians together across denominational and racial barriers. She is single and lives, for the time being, in Elgin, Illinois.

Accidentally or on Purpose?

> What a piece of work is a man! how noble in reason! how infinite in faculties! in form and moving how express and admirable! in action how like an angel! in apprehension how like a god! the beauty of the world! the paragon of animals! And yet, to me, what is this quintessence of dust?
>
> —William Shakespeare, Hamlet, act ii, sc. ii

• • •

What is the true nature of humanity? Is there some purpose for our being here? The Bible claims we were created in the image of God and that therefore we have ultimate significance. What does that mean? What difference does it make? On the next few pages are some ideas to help you explore those questions as well as some odds and ends to spark your thinking and your creativity in response.

Reflection

Finish these sentences with endings you've heard over and over again.

"Did anyone ever tell you look just like _____ ?"

"You know, you're just like _____ !"

"Why can't you be more like _____ ?"

How does it make you feel when you hear statements like these?

What would it mean to be told you look or act like Jesus? How would that make you feel?

If beauty is only skin deep, that means it can't be more than 3/16 of an inch thick.

Scripture Discovery

In the Image of God

*Man's superior dignity entitles him to the conquest of nature . . .
made possible through modern natural science. But modern natural
science seems to demonstrate that there is no essential difference
between man and nature, that man is simply a more organized and
rational form of slime.*

—*Francis Fukuyama,* The End of History and the Last Man

• • •

Are we just a more organized and rational form of slime? What are some of
the implications for our lives if this is true? The Bible says we're much more
valuable than that.

• Read Genesis 1:26-31. What does the Bible say sets humanity apart from
the animals?

• What role does this passage say God gave humanity? How have we fulfilled this role? How have we abused it?

• Check all the aspects you think are unique to human nature. Can modern natural science provide an explanation for these? Explain.

creativity   language   religion   self-awareness

culture   conscience   use of tools   science itself

other:

• How did God respond to His creation in verse 31? What does that mean to you?

• What do *you* think it means to be created in the "image of God"?

The excessive skepticism shown toward the Bible by important historical schools of the 18th and 19th centuries has been progressively discredited. Discovery after discovery has established the accuracy of innumerable details, and has brought increased recognition to the value of the Bible as a source of history. —William F. Albright, archaeologist

Reaction

When I consider your heavens, the work of your fingers, the moon and the stars, which you have set in place, what is man that you are mindful of him, the son of man that you care for him?

—Psalm 8:3, 4

• • •

What questions do you have about science and the Bible? What difference does it make what you believe about the nature of mankind? Draw a picture, make a mini-collage, write a poem or a monologue, etc. to express your opinion.

Leonardo da Vinci could draw with one hand and write with the other simultaneously.

Response

For we are God's workmanship [literally "poetry," in Greek], created in Christ Jesus to do good works, which God prepared in advance for us to do.

—Ephesians 2:10

• • •

We hear voices all around us that contradict what God says about us. From TV and magazines we get the idea that we only have value if we're beautiful, sexy, popular, or rich. From school, and sometimes parents, we can get the idea that we're only valuable if we're smart and successful and make others proud.

God says you make Him proud simply because He created you. As the bumper sticker says, "God don't make no junk!"

Look back over your Daily Markings and think about how you've seen God at work in your life. Write a prayer of response to God for something you learned this week.

Lord,

Amen

Daily Markings

For the week of _____

On these pages you can record significant events from your week and your feelings about them: a movie you saw, a conversation you had, a dream, etc. Use different colors, drawings, etc. to express how you felt about each event. When the week is over, look back to see how God was at work.

	Events	Feelings
Sun		
Mon		
Tue		

	Events	Feelings
Wed		
Thur		
Fri		
Sat		

Trash or Treasure?

Man is just a piece of trash in a universe that's running down.

—Samuel Beckett

• • •

Are not two sparrows sold for a penny? Yet not one of them will fall to the ground apart from the will of your Father. And even the very hairs of your head are all numbered. So don't be afraid; you are worth more than many sparrows.

—Jesus (Matt. 10:29-31)

• • •

The Bible says that not only are you valuable to God because He made you in His image, but also that you are of so much value to Him that He sent His One and Only Son to give His life in exchange for yours and buy you back from the control of the evil one so that He could have a relationship with you.

How much do you think you're worth? depends on the person. I think that I am worth every penny.

Reflection

For God so loved the world that he gave his one and only Son, that whoever believes in him shall not perish but have eternal life.

—John 3:16

• • •

When I think about Jesus dying on the cross it makes me feel:
(Check all that apply.)

X guilty as sin

__ like falling on my face in grateful repentance

X so sad that He had to suffer so much

X angry—I didn't ask Him to die for me!

X like I wish there was something I could do for Him

X angry that people could do that to an innocent man

__ a little better about the times I'm misunderstood

__ other: _____

Scripture Discovery

Bought Back

You are worthy to take the scroll and to open its seals, because you were slain, and with your blood you purchased men for God from every tribe and language and people and nation.

—Revelation 5:9

• • •

Our first parents, Adam and Eve enjoyed perfect friendship with God until they disobeyed His direct warning and ate the forbidden fruit. Genesis 3 records the results of their disobedience. Especially touching is the scene in verses 7-10. Read it, imagining yourself as Adam or Eve.

Do you hear God calling to you in verse 9? Imagine it. Go for a walk alone in a woods, a park, or a busy street and listen in your heart to God's words, "Where are you?"

God is still calling "Where are you?" to every man, woman, and child in the world. The whole Bible is the story of God's search and rescue plan for humanity. This plan culminated at the cross, which is where each of us must go because "all have sinned and fall short of the glory of God" (Romans 3:23).

> *You see, at just the right time, when we were still powerless, Christ died for the ungodly. Very rarely will anyone die for a righteous man, though for a good man someone might possibly dare to die. But God demonstrates his own love for us in this: While we were still sinners, Christ died for us.*
>
> *—Romans 5:6-8*

• • •

Why?

For further thought:

What does the cross show about our condition? What does it show about our worth? Why does the apostle Paul talk about the "offense of the cross" (Galatians 5:11 and I Corinthians 1:23)?

Written over a 1,600 year time-span, by over 40 different authors from all walks of life, on three continents, in three languages, covering all kinds of controversial topics, in various styles of literature, the Bible displays a remarkable unity. It is all one story—God's redemption of mankind. "The 'Paradise Lost' of Genesis becomes the 'Paradise Regained' of Revelation."

Reaction

Jesus said, "I have come to seek and to save that which was lost." Read the parable of the Lost Sheep in Luke 15:1-7 and use your creativity to journal your reaction.

The sound you hear when you hold a seashell to your ear is the echo of your own blood pulsing in your ear.

Response

The kingdom of heaven is like treasure hidden in a field. When a man found it, he hid it again, and then in his joy went and sold all he had and bought that field.

—Matthew 13:44

• • •

There's a double meaning in this parable. Express your thoughts on your own worth to God; then on what is really valuable to you. What is the kingdom of heaven worth to you?

Lord,

The kingdom of heaven worth to me is where we go when we are dead.

Amen

Spiders have transparent blood.

Daily Markings

For the week of <u>January 15</u>

	Events	Feelings
Sun	I went to church.	I feel good becau I missed a lot of people.
Mon	I went to school and watched 3 hours of basketball games	I liked school and liked to watch Girls Basketball games especially the players.
Tue	I worked for 8 hours,	I liked the money and met some nice friends.

	Events	Feelings
Wed	I went to school.	I liked the school because of my first choice.
Thur	I worked for 8 hours	I need the money for ~~a~~ schooling, buying gifts, and ~~money~~ buy miscellaneous for myself.
Fri	I worked for 8 hours.	I need the money.
Sat	Nothing	

Meaningless or Meaningful?

I believe in the immortality of the soul because I have within me immortal longings.

—Helen Keller

• • •

I have seen all the things that are done under the sun; all of them are meaningless, a chasing after the wind.

—Ecclesiastes 1:14

• • •

One of our greatest needs as human beings is to have a sense of purpose in life. Do you ever ask, what am I here for?

The Bible affirms that you are here for a purpose. You may never be famous. You may not be "the best" at anything. You may or may not make a lot of money in your life, but there is a reason for your being on planet Earth at this particular time, in this particular place, with these particular relationships as part of your life.

Do you believe that? Part of the adventure of being a Christian is getting little glimpses from time-to-time as to what that specific purpose may be.

Reflection

Have you ever thought of why you were born who you are and not some-body else? Maybe you wish you had been born into better, easier, happier circumstances. God knows. In your own way, reflect on these questions. Any clue as what purpose there may be for you being who you are?

Mirror, Mirror, on the wall,

Why am I who I am at all?

Scripture Discovery
A Plan and a Purpose

Question: What is the chief end of man?

Answer: To glorify God and enjoy him forever.

—The Westminster Catechism

• • •

How does this answer grab you? | Anything surprising about it?

We are suppose to tell his | no
word to other people.

God does have a plan, not just for you, but for the whole universe. You are a part of it. Examine the passage that follows to get a clue about what that purpose is, and who will benefit from it. Did the Westminster Catechism get it right? If so, how can this answer work out in daily living? yes, to tell other people that God died for you and me.

No fundamental doctrine of the Christian faith rests on a disputed reading [in the ancient texts of the Bible]. In substance the text of the Bible is certain: Especially is this the case with the N.T. The number of quotations from it in the oldest writers of the Church, is so large that it is practically certain that the true reading of every doubtful passage is preserved in some one or other of these ancient authorities. This can be said of no other ancient book in the world.

In him we have redemption through his blood, the forgiveness of sins, in accordance with the riches of God's grace that he lavished on us with all wisdom and understanding. And he made known to us (the mystery of his will) according to his good pleasure, which he purposed in Christ, to be put into effect when the times will have reached their fulfillment—to bring all things in heaven and on earth together under one head, even Christ.

In him we were also chosen, having been predestined <u>according to the plan of him who works out everything in conformity with the purpose of his will</u>, in order that we, who were the first to hope in Christ, might be for the praise of his glory. And you also were included in Christ when you heard the word of truth, the gospel of your salvation.

—Ephesians 1:7-13

• • •

• What does "redemption" mean? Sins our forgiven

• Underline specific words or phrases in the text that indicate that God has a plan for the world.

• Circle the phrase where "the mystery of his will" is revealed. What does that mean?

• Put brackets around the phrases that indicate the scope of God's plan (that means how much is covered by it).

• What are the privileges of those who believe in Christ? they say we go to heaven redemption

• What are believers predestined to or chosen for? Circle the answer that's given in the text. What does this answer mean to you?

Reaction

> How did you react personally to the text? What questions or problems does it raise for you? Write your own statement about the meaning of life.

I am lost Enjoy life while you can

On a hot summer day, the inside temperature of a cucumber is 20 degrees cooler than air temperature.

Response

Try this form to provide structure for your prayers.

My Part

Praise I get through school.

Admit I am a good student.

Requests that I pass Writing I.

Thanks for saying to turn other cheek.

God's Part

Listening: Meditate on Isaiah 40:21-31 and listen for what God has to say to you.

Messages: Reflect back over your week. What do you think the Lord wants to say to you?

Prayer format thanks to:

Wild Things Happen When I Pray by Becky Tirabassi, Zondervan, 1993.

Daily Markings

For the week of <u>January 22</u>

	Events	Feelings
Sun	I went to church.	Now, I like going to church.
Mon	I went to school.	I like this school (academics).
Tue	I went to work. Then, I went to a Girls Basketball game.	I need the money. I wanted a girl's address that made me mad.

	Events	Feelings
Wed	I went to school (again).	I always meet new people.
Thur	I went to work. Then, I went to get a haircut.	I like the money. I like the beautician because she will cut how you wanted cut.
Fri	I went to work.	I like the money a lot.
Sat	I went to the game against Bremen.	I like to socialize with people.

What's to Look Forward To?

And now the wheels of heaven stop; you feel the devil's riding crop. Get ready for the future: it is murder.

— Leonard Cohen, "The Future"

• • •

Dear friends, now we are children of God, and what we will be has not yet been made known. But we know that when he appears, we shall be like him, for we shall see him as he is. Everyone who has this hope in him purifies himself, just as he is pure.

—I John 3:2, 3

• • •

Karl Marx called religion "the opiate of the masses," assuming it would eventually die out as the quality of life in this world improved.

The lessons of history have proven Marx wrong in many ways, not the least in his view of religion. While technology has improved the quality of our lives physically, it has not not succeeded in overcoming human misery. Religion has not died out either, despite the modern bias against it. But Christianity rests on something more than wishful thinking about a better life in the hereafter, anyway. Christian hope rests on a fact of history—the resurrection of Jesus Christ.

Reflection

List some of the things you most look forward to. What is it that makes each worth waiting for? For example:

My birthday ♥ presents in February 1995

Christmas CD's

Getting married knowing what I like in a girl as friends. It could be 4-6 years down the road.

Imagine you are 81 years old looking back on your life. How do you feel? old

What is it that has made your life worthwhile? people who care about me

How do you feel about your impending death? What then?
I do not want to looking for my death. nothing, we can do about it

Scripture Discovery

Wishful Thinking?

I consider that our present sufferings are not worth comparing with the glory that will be revealed in us. The creation waits in eager expectation for the sons of God to be revealed.

—Romans 8:18, 19

• • •

What is the "Christian hope"?

The apostle Paul believed so strongly in the actual, physical resurrection of Christ that he said, "If only for *this* life we have hope in Christ, we are to be pitied more than all men." In other words, if this weren't true, I'd be outa here. Later in the same discussion he exclaimed, "If I fought wild beasts in Ephesus [referring to the hardships he endured spreading the Gospel] for merely human reasons, what have I gained? If the dead are not raised, 'Let us eat and drink, for tomorrow we die'" (I Corinthians 15:19, 32).

Study chapter 15 of I Corinthians.

• Why does Paul keep saying, "according to the Scriptures"? (Look up Isaiah 53, especially verses 10 and 11; see also Psalms 16 and 22.) He wants us to refer to the Bible more often and come to church also.

• Why was it so important to Paul to prove that Christ actually rose from the dead? Can't you be a good Christian and not believe that? Which of his points carries the most weight? People did not believe Paul. I have no idea. I have to say verse 6.

• What is the significance of this one person coming back to life? How would Paul answer the "so what?" question? How do you answer it?

Read Romans 8:18-25.

• Define hope as it's used here. How is it different than wishful thinking? Without hope, then we will not be saved.

• What is the ultimate hope of the Christian? Describe it.

The Old Testament contains over 300 references to the Messiah that were fulfilled in Jesus, 60 of which are very specific and detailed. The odds that just 8 of these could be fulfilled in one man are 1 in 10 to the 17th power (1,000,000,000,000,000,000).

Reaction

Is all this talk about resurrection and hope of heaven just

Pie in the Sky By and By?

Why?

What's the difference between having hope and just having

Fire Insurance?

André Crouch once sang, "If Heaven never was promised to me, neither God's House to live eternally, it's been worth just having the Lord in my life. I was living in a world of darkness; He brought me the light." Do you agree, or would you rather say

All This, and Heaven Too?

Response

First of all, you must understand that in the last days scoffers will come, scoffing and following their own evil desires. They will say, "Where is this 'coming' he promised? Ever since our fathers died, everything goes on as it has since the beginning . . ."

But the day of the Lord will come like a thief. The heavens will disappear with a roar; the elements will be destroyed by fire, and the earth and everything in it will be laid bare . . .

But in keeping with his promise we are looking forward to a new heaven and new earth, the home of righteousness.

So then, dear friends, since you are looking forward to this, make every effort to be found spotless, blameless and at peace with him.

—II Peter 3:3, 10, 14

• • •

If this is so, what do you need to say to God today?

God,

Amen

1000 AD—several unsuccessful attempts are made to fly or float in air.

Daily Markings

For the week of <u>February 1⁵</u>

	Events	Feelings
Sun	I went to church.	Now, I am starting to like church.
Mon	I went to school.	There are some peope that I like.
Tue	I went to work.	I made some new friends at work and I need the money.

	Events	Feelings
Wed	I went to school.	I need an education.
Thur	I went to work.	I need the money and I met some new friends at work.
Fri	I went to work.	I need the money and I met some new friends at work.
Sat	I went to a basketball game.	I did not like the game but I had fun talking to some of the spectators.

WEEK 5

The Difference It Makes

We live on the surface of "things"; our lives are easily described, but rarely understood, busy but going nowhere in particular. . . . We are like astronauts, each in our own space-suit, orbiting the earth.

—James Houston, The Heart's Desire

• • •

Joy is the gigantic secret of the Christian.

—G. K. Chesterton

• • •

Some people try to peddle Christianity as the solution to all of life's problems. But if you're a Christian, you've probably already discovered that you have the same doubts, questions, anxieties, and struggles as everybody else.

So where is this joy? This peace we're promised? What difference does it make?

The Bible does offer the promise of a better quality of life, but it doesn't come naturally, and it doesn't come overnight.

Reflection

But the fruit of the Spirit is love, joy, peace, patience, kindness, goodness, faithfulness, gentleness and self-control. Against such things there is no law.

—Galatians 5:22

• • •

Fruit Picking

Check out what's growing on the tree of your life. For instance, has love ripened in you or are you still pretty green with things like jealousy or selfishness? Is joy blossoming in your heart? What about goodness? Self-control? Etc. Describe the fruit that's growing in your life.

What quality of the Holy Spirit from Galatians 5:22 do you most need in your life right now?

Scripture Discovery

That Extra Dimension

I had motives for not wanting the world to have meaning; consequently assumed that it had none, and was able without any difficulty to find satisfying reasons for this assumption. The philosopher who finds no meaning in the world is not concerned exclusively with a problem in pure metaphysics, he is also concerned to prove that there is no valid reason why he personally should not do as he wants to do. . . . For myself, the philosophy of meaninglessness was essentially an instrument of liberation, sexual and political.

—Aldous Huxley

• • •

NOT QUITE
PERFECT

SORRY,
NO DICE

GETTING THERE!

OKAY,
I GUESS

SO, SO

COULD BE
BETTER

NEEDS
IMPROVEMENT

WEAK

CRUMMY

ROTTEN

The Bible says our lives matter. We are significant to God, and He has a purpose for our lives. There is always a connection between who we are and what we do—between identity and meaning, purpose and responsibility—but if we get things backward, we're in trouble. If we try to find our identity and value by what we do, we will never get away from a feeling of not measuring up. That's because what we do can only flow from who we are—children of God, made in His image, of so much value that He would send His Son to buy us back with the price of His own blood.

Read 1 Peter 2:9-12.

• What are the duties of a priest? Who are Christians supposed to serve as priests?

• Which do you feel more like—part of a holy nation, or an alien and stranger in the world? How can you be both?

• What is holiness? If Christians are already a "holy nation," why does Peter urge them to act holy?

• Do you agree that your desires war against your soul? How?

Read Romans 8:6-11.

• How can we win this war with our own desires? How can we be holy? What, or rather, who is it that can make the difference in our lives?

Ancient Jewish scribes called Massoretes who copied the Bible were so careful that they numbered the verses, words, and letters of every book. They calculated the middle word and the middle letter of each line; then counted back so that they could detect even the most minute of errors.

Reaction

Ideas:

• Make a collage to illustrate how you view your true significance.

• Write a statement of what you now believe about yourself, and the part that faith now plays in your life.

• Write or doodle some of the honest questions and struggles you still have. What's the next step in your quest?

Response

Therefore, I urge you, brothers, in view of God's mercy, to offer your bodies as living sacrifices, holy and pleasing to God—this is your spiritual act of worship. Do not conform any longer to the pattern of this world, but be transformed by the renewing of your mind. Then you will be able to test and approve what God's will is—his good, pleasing and perfect will.

—Romans 12:1, 2

• • •

My Part

Praise

Admit

Requests

Thanks

God's Part

Listening: Meditate on the Twenty Third Psalm until you hear the Lord speaking in your heart.

Messages:

Daily Markings

For the week of <u>February 19</u>

Events   Feelings

Sun I went to church.

Mon I went to ~~work~~ school.

Tue I went to work.

	Events	Feelings

Wed I went to school.

Thur I went to work.

Fri I went to work.

Sat

UNIT Two

One of a Kind

Exploring My Uniqueness

by Laurel Edison

Imagine a world populated with billions of people identical to yourself. They share your appearance and personality; your strengths and weaknesses. Whenever you think a thought, laugh or cry, billions of "yous" join in.

Leave the world of sameness and travel to another world—a world inhabited by beings totally different from yourself. When you feel love or pain, no one understands because these emotions do not exist for them.

You might as well exist in a vacuum.

We need each other. Indeed, it is only in the context of relationships that we realize our own uniqueness. This uniqueness is reason to celebrate. It brings richness and variety to our lives. Yet all too often our differences divide us. Why? Perhaps we fear that we might lose those qualities that distinguish us from others.

Why did God make you unique? Can the individual and the community coexist? What do you think? What does God say? Use this journal to explore those questions.

Laurel Edison was living at home, working in a floral shop in Ludington, Michigan when she wrote this. She is now working as a receptionist for her Congressman in Washington, D. C. Laurel is fluent in German, having studied at Tübingen University in Germany. She graduated from the University of Michigan, where as part of her program she taught creative writing in prisons.

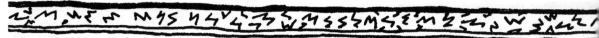

WEEK 6 ME I AM

I am the only ME I AM
who qualifies as me;
No ME I AM has been before,
and none will ever be.

No other ME I AM can feel
the feelings I've within;
no other ME I AM can fit
precisely in my skin.

There is no other ME I AM
who thinks the thoughts I do;
the world contains one ME I AM,
there is no room for two.

I am the only ME I AM
this earth shall ever see;
that ME I AM I always am
is no one else but ME!
— *Jack Prelutsky,* The Random House Book of Poetry for Children

• • •

You are the only you you are. Like fingerprints, though there are similarities and common types, our personalities are unique. God has created as many personalities as He has individuals, and He loves them all.

Reflection

Pick several ice cream flavors that best describe your personality. Explain why.

Scripture Discovery

A Tapestry

Individuality is all elbows, it separates and isolates. . . . [It] counterfeits personality as lust counterfeits love. . . . It is the continual assertion of individuality that hinders our spiritual life more than anything else.

Personality is that peculiar, incalculable thing that is meant when we speak of ourselves as distinct from everyone else.

—Oswald Chambers

• • •

Shepherds, mothers, kings, fishermen, tax collectors, doctors, scholars. Christ's followers did not become a group of clones. They retained their personalities, but relinquished individualism. Outspoken, quiet, impetuous, reflective, practical. God called them all into His service and commanded them to allow Him to be their common denominator.

Read Romans 15:1-7 and discover God's plan for community life. Who are the strong? the weak? To which group do you belong?

How should the strong "bear with the failings of the weak"? What purpose might this "bearing with" serve?

Where does the "spirit of unity" come from? What should it produce?

What kind of acceptance do you expect from others? from God? On what basis does Christ accept us? Read Titus 3:3-8.

For further thought:

Are we what we do? How closely is our action tied to our being? Is it possible to accept a person without accepting his/her behavior?

Reaction

Differences can be refreshing as well as irritating. Think of someone who gets on your nerves. What things about his or her personality irritate you? Why? Are there differences you find refreshing?

Einstein's brain is stored in a mason jar in a Wichita, Kansas laboratory.

Response

You, my brothers, were called to be free. But do not use your free-dom to indulge the sinful nature; rather, serve one another in love.

—Galatians 5:13

• • •

God gives us unique personalities and calls us to freedom. He also commands us to love one another and to live harmoniously. Respond to Him.

Lord,

Amen

Daily Markings

For the week of _____

	Events	Feelings
Sun		
Mon		
Tue		

	Events	Feelings
Wed		
Thur		
Fri		
Sat		

WEEK 7

Am I Weak? Am I Strong?

In all our weaknesses, we have one element of strength if we recognize it. Here, as in other things, knowledge of danger is often the best means of safety.

—E. P. Rose, New Dictionary of Thoughts

• • •

If scientists were to develop an immunization against weakness, who would not clamor for the shot? In our minds weakness equals worthlessness. Attempting to prove our value we hide our weaknesses behind our strengths, trembling lest they be discovered—trembling lest they remain undiscovered.

Do you know your own strength? What are your weaknesses? In II Corinthians 12:10 the apostle Paul boasts of his weakness saying, "For when I am weak, then I am strong." Could weakness be a strength? Could strength be a weakness?

Reflection

Edinburgh Castle in Scotland has only been captured once in history. Thought to be impregnable where it rises out of sheer rock on one side, no sentries were placed there. Only the point of its accessibility was guarded. One night, the enemy quietly scaled the rock and jumped over the wall, easily subduing the garrison and taking the castle.

Have you ever been taken by surprise at just the point you thought was your strongest? How can you guard against your strengths becoming weaknesses?

Ounce for ounce, a bumblebee is 150 times stronger than an elephant.

Scripture Discovery

Power Perfected in Weakness

Three times I pleaded with the Lord to take it away from me. But he said to me, "My grace is sufficient for you, for my power is made perfect in weakness."

—II Corinthians 12:8, 9a

• • •

God often chose the "weak things of the world to shame the strong" (I Corinthians 1:27): the boy David conquered the giant Goliath with a slingshot and stone; the Israelites marched around Jericho and its walls crumbled; Jesus came to our world as an infant and conquered sin and death by His sacrifice on the cross.

Read Exodus 3:7-12.

What is God's response to the "cry of the Israelites"?

Does Moses' question in verse 11 seem unreasonable to you? How might you have responded?

What do you notice about the way God answers Moses' question?

Read Exodus 4:10-12.

What concerns Moses?

How does God respond? Why?

Reaction

My strength without God becomes weakness. My weakness given to God becomes strength.

How can this be? Write a short skit/dialogue or a poem expressing your ideas.

Response

Look to the Lord and his strength; seek his face always.

—Psalm 105:4

. . . in quietness and trust is your strength. . .   *—Isaiah 30:15*

The Sovereign Lord is my strength; he makes my feet like the feet of a deer, he enables me to go on the heights.

—Habakkuk 3:19

• • •

Talk to God about your strengths and weaknesses and how your thinking has changed this week.

Lord,

Amen

Daily Markings

For the week of _____

	Events	Feelings
Sun		
Mon		
Tue		

	Events	Feelings
Wed		
Thur		
Fri		
Sat		

WEEK 8

What's My Contribution?

He was a football player/ of the first degree/ He was a lousy student/ But they let him be/ . . . Ten years later he's just a bore.

—Phil Madeira, "Life After High School,"
from the album Attitude by Kenny Marks

Then Moses said to the Israelites, "See, the Lord has chosen Bezalel . . . and he has filled him with the Spirit of God, with skill, ability and knowledge in all kinds of crafts—to make artistic designs . . ."

—Exodus 35:30-32

• • •

Our sense of self-worth is intimately tied to the question, "Do I have something meaningful to give?" Bezalel was a talented craftsman. What talents do you possess? The dictionary defines talent as "a gift committed to one's trust to use and improve." If talent is a gift, who is the giver? Our talents should bless others and bring God glory.

Reflection

What do you enjoy doing? What do you think you do well? Make a list.

Do you think others believe you have something to offer? What have you heard people say about your talents? If you're not sure, ask a friend.

Scripture Discovery

The Gifts and the Giver

There are different kinds of gifts, but the same Spirit. There are different kinds of service, but the same Lord. There are different kinds of working, but the same God works all of them in all men.

—*I Corinthians 12:4-6*

• • •

On several occasions Paul teaches about spiritual gifts, gifts given to those who have chosen to follow Christ. What are these gifts and how do they reflect the character of the Giver? For what purpose does the Spirit give these gifts? How do people discover their gifts?

Read Romans 12:3-8.

What does Paul mean when he writes, "think of yourself with sober judgment"? How does this fit in with what our culture says about self-esteem?

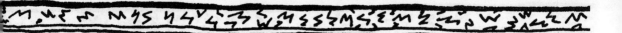

Paul compares those who are in Christ to the members of a body and suggests in verse 5 that "each member belongs to all the others"? What are the implications of this statement? Reflect on the challenges, responsibilities, benefits, and sacrifices of this kind of inter-relatedness.

What are the different gifts? What do they have in common?

A man who was merely a man and said the sort of things Jesus said would not be a great moral teacher. He would either be a lunatic—on a level with the man who says he is a poached egg—or else he would be a Devil of Hell. You must make your choice. Either this man was, and is, the Son of God: or else a madman or something worse. You can shut Him up for a fool, you can spit at Him and kill Him as a demon; or you can fall at His feet and call Him Lord and God. But let us not come up with any patronising nonsense about His being a great moral teacher. He has not left that open to us. He did not intend to. —C. S. Lewis, *Mere Christianity*

Reaction

MY TALENT

Read the parable of the talents in Matthew 25:14-30. Use your creativity to respond to this teaching.

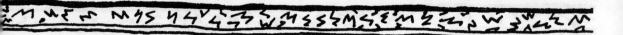

Response

Now to each one the manifestation of the Spirit is given for the common good.

—*I Corinthians 12:7*

• • •

What can you offer to God? If you're not sure what talents, abilities, or gifts God's given you, ask Him to show you.

Lord,

Amen

Daily Markings

For the week of _____

	Events	Feelings
Sun		
Mon		
Tue		

Events   Feelings

Wed

Thur

Fri

Sat

Do Fairy Tales Come True?

Nothing happens unless first a dream.

—Carl Sandburg

I dreamed a dream in time gone by,/ when hope was high and life worth living./ I dreamed that love would never die,/ I dreamed that God would be forgiving. . . . I had a dream that my life would be,/ So different from this hell I'm living./ So different now from what it seemed./ Now life has killed the dream I dreamed.

—Fantine in Les Miserables; *from "I Dreamed a Dream" by Alain Boublil*

• • •

Do dreams transform reality or does reality kill dreams? Perhaps it depends on the nature of our dreams and their relationship to the realities that confront us. In what ways can dreams be positive? negative?

How does God fit into your dreams and goals?

Reflection

What we dream about influences who we will become.

My Dreams . . .	**These Dreams Make Me Feel . . .**
career	wistful
fame	cynical
marriage	vulnerable
happiness	determined

Explain.

Humans are the only animals that cry.

Scripture Discovery
God Wants to Guide You

> *. . . because God loves us so much, He often guides us by planting His own lovely dream in the barren soil of a human heart. When the dream has matured and the time for its fulfillment is ripe, to our astonishment and delight, we find that God's will has become our will and our will God's.*
>
> —Catherine Marshall, Meeting God at Every Turn

• • •

Do you seek God's plans and dreams for you, or do you bring Him your dream list and beg for His heavenly endorsement?

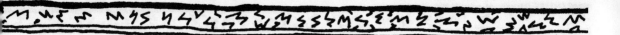

Read Psalm 37:4.

Define "delight."

How might you take delight in the Lord? What characteristics of God delight you? Is there anything about God that doesn't delight you?

Is there any changing going on in this verse? If so, who or what is doing the changing?

". . . he will give you the desires of your heart." What does this mean? Is this verse a wish-fulfillment formula?

What are the desires of your heart? Would the act of delighting yourself in the Lord alter any of these desires?

French philosopher Voltaire [1694–1778] once boasted that Christianity and the Bible would be extinct in 100 years. Fifty years after his death the Geneva Bible Society was using his house and printing press to print Bibles.

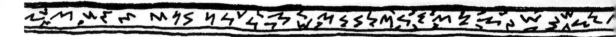

Reaction

Our dreams are often noble. They become tainted only as we pursue them, for we are incapable of making them real on our own. Hoping to realize dreams of love, peace, security and joy, we pursue romance, sex, pleasure, money, and prestige. And we are disappointed. In this we fail to recognize that God has already offered us that for which we dream in the person of His Son Jesus Christ.

Christ's character. Your dreams. Combine these two concepts creatively.

Response

"For I know the plans I have for you," declares the Lord, "plans to prosper you and not to harm you, plans to give you hope and a future."

—Jeremiah 29:11

. . .

Do you dare to seek God's plan for you even if it might mean sacrificing some of your own dreams? Respond.

Lord,

Amen

Voltaire's last words: "I am abandoned by God and man. I shall go to hell! O Christ, O Jesus Christ!"

Daily Markings

For the week of _____

Events Feelings

Sun

Mon

Tue

	Events	Feelings
Wed		
Thur		
Fri		
Sat		

WEEK 10 Glory Be!

Glory be to God for dappled things—
For skies of couple-colour as a brinded cow;
For rose-moles all in stipple upon trout that swim;
Fresh-firecoal chestnut-falls; finches' wings;
Landscape plotted and pieced—fold, fallow, and plough;
And áll trádes, their gear and tackle and trim.

All things counter, original, spare, strange;
Whatever is fickle, freckled (who knows how?)
With swift, slow; sweet, sour; adazzle, dim;
He fathers-forth whose beauty is past change:
Praise him.

—Gerard Manley Hopkins, "Pied Beauty"

• • •

Who or what is the source of your uniqueness? According to the Bible, God is. Although we have smudged—pretty badly—God's image, we still reflect His nature. Our uniqueness testifies to His abounding creativity. Praise Him!

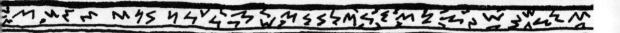

Reflection

. . . Thank heaven you're romantic and irascible, I'm opinionated in my impulsiveness. Thank God we can lean together in our failing — a rusty trellis propping a thorned rose.

—Luci Shaw, "Spice"

• • •

Is variety really the spice of life, or is it merely irritating? How does our uniqueness enhance our world? What problems does it create?

Think about someone you know well. What makes him or her unique? How are your friends different from you?

Scripture Discovery

Celebrate

Each one of us is as irreplaceable as a rare specimen in a collection.

—Ernesto Cardenal

• • •

You are in an art museum. A painting catches your eye. The use of lighting and color is exquisite. Do you praise the painting for its remarkable achievements? No. It is the artist who deserves your praise.

We are God's workmanship, a work of art, His masterpiece. Do you believe this? You are precious in God's eyes and He loves you. When we choose to accept His gift of love through Jesus Christ, He gives us the right to become His children.

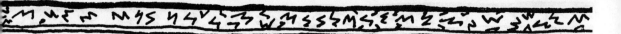

Read and meditate on the following Scripture passages:

Psalm 139

Ephesians 2:10

Acts 17:28

I John 3:1, 2

What do you learn about yourself in these verses? Make a list and comment.

Reaction

I am what I am and that's all that I am.

—*Popeye, "The Popeye Show"*

• • •

Ideas:

Praise God for creating you by composing your own psalm (perhaps you could set it to music). Tape a picture of yourself on this page and write a description of your unique qualities and abilities.

Response

Take a walk or think about your favorite outdoor spot. Think about the uniqueness all around you. Ask God how He wants you to use the unique abilities He's given you. Express your heart to Him in prayer.

Lord,

The average man's beard has about thirteen thousand whiskers.

Amen

Daily Markings

For the week of _____

	Events	Feelings
Sun		
Mon		
Tue		

	Events	Feelings
Wed		
Thur		
Fri		
Sat		

⸬Three
I'm Not Alone:

Exploring My Connectedness with Others

by Kelly Peavey

You've heard it said, "Look out for number one. Make a life for yourself. If you don't look out for yourself, no one else will." The world around us is pushing for independence and self. And there are times when the world seems right. Times when you feel you'd be better off living alone on some island, away from the hassles and pain of dealing with people day in and day out.

But if satisfaction is found in doing things on our own, why do we long for relationships—a true friend, an understanding parent, or a caring girl-friend or boyfriend? Somehow, making it in the world on our own comes up short of fulfilling our deepest desires for closeness and a sense of belonging.

The Bible offers some explanations about why we aren't content to be alone. It says God created us for relationships—with Him and with others. And even if you don't openly admit to wanting to be close to God, the desire to be known and to know others intimately is forever a part of your makeup. What's more, God designed a way for people to fulfill their longings to be loved and to love others.

You'll have a chance to see what the Bible says about all of this, as well as explore your own thoughts and feelings as you use this journal. Write your honest reactions, discover what the Bible has to say, and learn more about who you are.

Kelly Peavey is a former high school teacher who has worked with youth for over ten years. Now married and a mother of two, Kelly is a freelance writer. She has a degree in education from Texas Tech University and now lives in Plaistow, New Hampshire, where she is active in lay ministry in her church.

No Man Is an Island

I've built walls,
A fortress steep and mighty,
That none may penetrate.
I have no need for friendship;
friendship causes pain.
Its laughter and its loving I disdain.
        I am a rock.
        I am an island.

                    —Paul Simon, "I Am a Rock," 1968

• • •

The above song by Paul Simon, goes on to say "A rock feels no pain; and an island never cries." But is this true? Does solitude protect us from pain? Can we alleviate the humiliation of rejection, the despair of misunderstandings, and the frustration of disagreements by isolating ourselves from others? Can we truly fulfill the desires of our hearts on our own?

Reflection

We're All Connected

Everyone is a member of a number of groups: family, neighborhood, school, nation, human race, etc. Fill in your relationship network, starting with those closest to you emotionally. Any gaps?

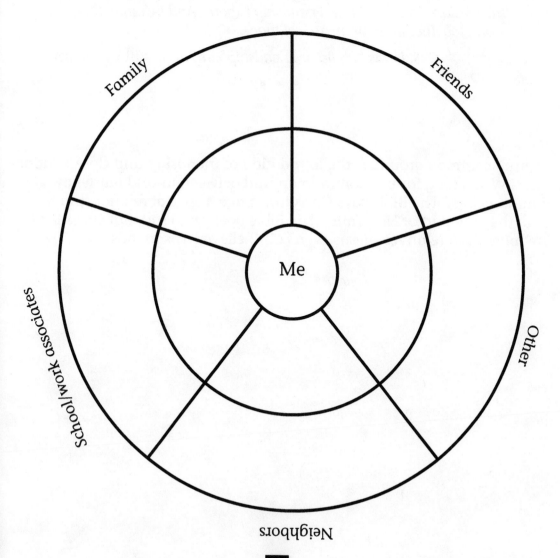

Scripture Discovery

I Have Called You Friends

It is when two such persons discover one another, when, whether with immense difficulties and semi-articulate fumblings or with what would seem to us amazing and elliptical speed, they share their vision—it is then that Friendship is born. And instantly they stand together in an immense solitude.

—C. S. Lewis, *"Philia or Friendship" in* The Joyful Christian

• • •

Sharing common ground is the foundation of friendship and close relationships. We all long for this common ground between us and our fellow human beings. The Bible says Christians have a special relationship to God; they are part of His family. The Bible goes on to say that Christians are more than relatives—Jesus even calls believers His friends.

• Read John 15:9-15. How does Jesus describe His love for the disciples?

• According to this passage, how can the disciples remain in the love of Jesus? Why did Jesus share this truth with them?

• What is Jesus' command to the disciples? Do you think this is a difficult command to keep? Explain.

• Why does Jesus call the disciples friends?

• How important is it to you to have Jesus call you friend?

For further thought:

What responsibilities do you think go along with being called Jesus' friend?

If we truly are Jesus' friends, how should we treat one another?

Reaction

The reason it's hard for me to reach out to others or bear my soul is . . .

When someone rejects me or betrays my confidence, I feel . . .

When someone shares his/her feelings and thoughts with me, I feel . . .

GOD WANTS TO SHARE HIS
PERSONAL THOUGHTS WITH YOU.

Response

God sets the lonely in families, he leads forth the prisoners with singing; but the rebellious live in a sun-scorched land.

—*Psalm 68:6*

How great is the love the Father has lavished on us, that we should be called children of God!

—*I John 3:1a*

• • •

There is little comfort in loneliness and isolation. Day in and day out, making it on your own will leave your soul dry as a desert. Deep within our hearts we long to be understood. God designed us with this need and provided love to fill it—love for one another and most of all Him. Think about the relationships in your life. Reflect on how God has or has not filled your need to be loved. Respond in prayer.

God,

Amen

A horse can look ahead with one eye and back with the other.

Daily Markings

For the week of _____

	Events	Feelings
Sun		
Mon		
Tue		

	Events	Feelings
Wed		
Thur		
Fri		
Sat		

WEEK 12 Give and Take

We require individualism which does not wall man off from community; we require community which sustains but does not suffocate the individual.

—Arthur M. Schlesinger

• • •

The way you view the world affects how you live your life and interact with others. Are you a loner or a team player?

Getting along together does not mean we all have to look, walk, and talk alike. God created each individual with unique personalities and talents. But when these diverse individuals are brought together through faith in Jesus Christ, the Bible says they become members of God's family and part of His body, the church. Strange concept, eh? What do you think it means?

Reflection

Harmony is pure love, for love is complete agreement.

—*Lope De Vega*

• • •

Is this true? Harmony and love are not easy to define, let alone live out. Write your own definitions.

Harmony:

Love:

Scripture Discovery
Body Basics

The body is a unit, though it is made up of many parts; and though all its parts are many, they form one body. So it is with Christ.

—*I Corinthians 12:12*

• • •

According to the Bible, the church is not just an organization, it's an organism. Part of the Christian's growth in Christ is the process of moving from a self-centered perspective to unity and love as each individual performs his or her own part in connection with the whole.

Still, tolerating diversity within the church is not easy. The Bible offers some basic principles to help people get along and function like a body.

• Read Ephesians 4:1-6. According to this passage, how are Christians supposed to treat each other? Why?

• Why do you think Paul stresses the word "one" in verses 4-6?

• Do you think unity is that important? Explain.

• What efforts could you make to bring unity and peace to your relationships?

And on the day called Sunday there is a gathering together to one place of all those who live in cities or in the country, and the memoirs of the apostles or the writings of the prophets are read. . . . Then when the reader has ceased the president presents admonition and invitation to the imitation of these good things. —Justin Martyr (100–165 A.D.)

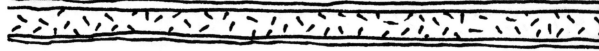

Reaction

Behold, how good and how pleasant it is for brethren to dwell together in unity!

—Psalm 133:1 (KJV)

• • •

How do you explain the difference between the ideal of unity in the body of Christ with the reality you see around you among Christians and different churches?

If unity among Christians were more of a reality, what would that look like, and what would it say to you? Why?

Response

There are different kinds of gifts, but the same Spirit.
There are different kinds of service, but the same Lord.
There are different kinds of working, but the same God works
all of them in all men.

—I Corinthians 12:4-6

• • •

God has made you unique, just as He has given others their own special qualities. Take time to thank God for the unique qualities He has given you and those around you. Ask Him to show you how you can love those who are different from you.

Lord,

Baboons can't throw overhand.

Amen

Daily Markings

For the week of _____

	Events	Feelings
Sun		
Mon		
Tue		

	Events	Feelings
Wed		
Thur		
Fri		
Sat		

WEEK 13 Togetherness

Wouldn't you like to get away? Sometimes you have to go
Where everybody knows your name, and they're always glad you
  came.
You want to go where people know that people are all the same.
You want to go where everybody knows your name.

—*Theme song from "Cheers"*

• • •

People need people; it's part of our makeup. We long for a safe place where we are loved and valued for who we are. Where are those safe places? The neighborhood bar? The mall? Where can you go and be known, understood, accepted, and loved?

God intended the church to be that safe place, a place where people encourage, accept, and love one another. Do you believe the church today can be a place like that?

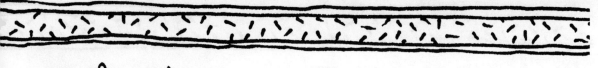

Reflection

Shared experience is the glue that bonds people together. When you get together with your close friends, what stories do you tell, what feelings do you remember? What comes to mind when you consider these bonds?

• humor/fun

• sorrow/suffering

• commitment/work

• other:

Scripture Discovery

Community Matters

When he had said this, he knelt down with all of them and prayed. They all wept as they embraced him and kissed him. What grieved them most was his statement that they would never see his face again. Then they accompanied him to the ship.

—Acts 20:36-38

Greet one another with a holy kiss.

—Romans 16:16a

• • •

Sometimes the apostle Paul gets a bum rap from modern readers. He seems so stern, so chauvinistic, even sexist. It's true, Paul was uncompromising, and some of the things he said are hard to understand. But there's another side. Romans 16 is a chapter most people just skim over, but it says a lot about the kind of a place the church was, and still can be. (And by the way, Paul had never actually been to Rome.)

• Read Romans 16. Jot down your observations about this list of people.

• What kinds of words does the apostle use to describe these relationships?

• What does that tell you about him, about them, about the church as a whole?

• Read verses 17-19. What warnings does Paul give the church at Rome? Why?

• On what basis could this diverse group of people experience such a sense of community? See verses 25-27.

A copy of the book of Isaiah dated 900 A.D. and held in the library of St. Petersburg was the oldest O.T. manuscript known until several scrolls were discovered near the Dead Sea in 1947. Among them was a copy of Isaiah dating back to 100 B.C. The 2 copies, written over 1,000 years apart, are virtually identical.

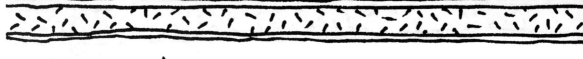

Reaction

Where two or three are gathered together in my name, there am I in the midst of them.

—Matthew 18:20 (KJV)

• • •

What would you expect it to be like if God were actually present with a group of people? Have you ever experienced such a thing? If so, describe it. If not, why do you think you haven't? Would you want to?

Besides humans, pigs are the only other mammal capable of getting sunburned.

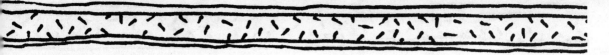

Response

By this all men will know that you are my disciples, if you love one another.

—*John 13:35*

• • •

God calls Christians to love one another. Love is more than a feeling; it involves action. Do your actions reflect love? Respond in prayer.

Lord,

Amen

Daily Markings

For the week of _____

	Events	Feelings
Sun		
Mon		
Tue		

Events   Feelings

Wed

Thur

Fri

Sat

Handle with Care!

Hell is—other people!

—J. P. Sartre

• • •

All of your strength is in your union.
All of your danger is in discord;
Therefore be at peace henceforward,
And as brothers live together.

—Henry Wadsworth Longfellow, The Song of Hiawatha

• • •

Someone has said, "I love mankind, it's people I can't stand." It's nice to talk about the idyllic early church when the people met together daily and held all things in common. But it didn't take long for problems to creep in, even in the earliest days of Christianity. Just read the book of Acts. Genuine Christian community, like marriage, takes work. It must be handled with care.

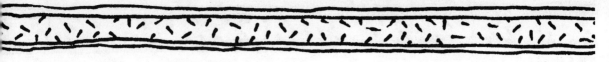

Reflection

I lay it down as a fact that if all men knew what others say of them, there would not be four friends in all the world.

—*Blaise Pascall,* Pensees

• • •

Ouch! What have you been saying about other people lately? Remember this bit of parental advice: "If you can't say something nice about someone, don't say anything at all." Think of something you shouldn't have said, and replace it with something more loving.

Mouth check!

What I could have/should have said.

Scripture Discovery

Acting Like Babies

What causes fights and quarrels among you? Don't they come from your desires that battle within you? You want something but don't get it. You kill and covet, but you cannot have what you want. You quarrel and fight. You do not have, because you do not ask God. When you ask, you do not receive, because you ask with wrong motives, that you may spend what you get on your pleasures. . . .

> *"God opposes the proud*
> *but gives grace to the humble."*

—James 4:1-3, 6

• • •

Conflict and opposition can destroy relationships. The New Testament writers saw the destruction that discord brought in the church and urgently warned church members to get along with each other. Time and again they urged the early church to resist arguments, hatred, rage, and other sins that cause division.

• What else can you think of that could bring division in the church?

• What relationship does pride have to quarrels and fights?

• Read I Corinthians 3:1-3. Why does the writer call the church members infants?

• What does he mean when he calls the Corinthians worldly?

• What do you think he meant when he talked about "milk" and "solid food"?

I have, for me at least, irrefutable evidence of the objective existence of the Person so moving me. When to this personal experience I add that of tens of thousands of living Christians, an unbroken line of them back to Christ, and when I find in the New Testament a manifold record of like experiences, together with a clear account of the origin and cause of them all. —E. Y. Mullins

Reaction

In your opinion, what is wrong with the church today? Any constructive ideas for improvement?

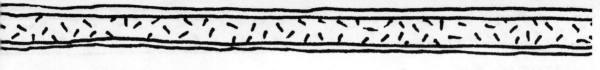

Response

If it is possible, as far as it depends on you, live at peace with everyone.

—Romans 12:18

• • •

It's easy to point the finger of blame at others for the discord in relationships. The difficulty lies in examining yourself and the areas you need to work on. The problem may not be yours, but you're the only one you can change. Pause a moment and reflect.

Lord,

I'm sorry . . .

Thank you . . .

Help me . . .

I praise you . . .

Amen

Daily Markings

For the week of _____

	Events	Feelings
Sun		
Mon		
Tue		

	Events	Feelings
Wed		
Thur		
Fri		
Sat		

WEEK 15
Building Blocks

Christian brotherhood is not an ideal which we must realize; it is rather a reality created by God in Christ in which we may participate.

—*Dietrich Bonhoeffer,* Life Together

• • •

To be sure, living together as a community in Christ is not easy. There are differences to overcome, qualities to learn to appreciate, and unique personalities and gifts to work with. However, as Bonhoeffer reminds us, it is a reality, a gift of God's grace through Jesus Christ. The building blocks of community are confession of sin, forgiveness, patience with each other, and most of all faith in Jesus Christ, who has promised to make His glory radiate through us.

Reflection

Let no debt remain outstanding, except the continuing debt to love one another, for he who loves his fellowman has fulfilled the law.

—Romans 13:8

• • •

• What relational debts do you have outstanding?

• How can you reconcile (pay) them?

Scripture Discovery

Dress for Success

Just as each of us has one body with many members, and these members do not all have the same function, so in Christ we who are many form one body, and each member belongs to all the others.

—Romans 12:4, 5

• • •

The Bible leaves no room for speculation on the value of the church. Scripture refers to the church as God's chosen people, the bride of Christ, and God's building to name a few. God calls His people together—no exceptions. Jews, Greeks, blacks, whites, rich, poor, Catholic, Protestant—all are called to unity in Christ Jesus.

And yet, this unity does not require Christians to lose their identity. In fact, the Bible is clear—God does not want a church full of Christian clones! The church is designed for unity in diversity.

Read Colossians 3:12-17.

• What are God's people to clothe themselves with? How does that happen?

• How are Christians supposed to act?

• How would doing everything in the name of Jesus affect the way you live?

P.S. Did you notice the description of God's people in verse 12—"holy and dearly loved"? Why is this important, or is it?

Studies show that churchgoers have lower blood pressure than others.

Reaction

Draw a cartoon, write a dialogue, or somehow creatively express how you've come to feel about the church.

Vincent van Gogh didn't start drawing till he was 27 years old.

Response

It is easily forgotten that the fellowship of Christian brethren is a gift of grace, a gift of the Kingdom of God that any day may be taken from us, that the time that still separates us from utter loneliness may be brief indeed. Therefore, let him who until now has had the privilege of living a common Christian life with other Christians praise God on his knees and declare: It is grace, nothing but grace that we are allowed to live in community with Christian brethren.

—Dietrich Bonhoeffer, Life Together

• • •

Respond in prayer.

Lord,

Amen

Daily Markings

For the week of _____

	Events	Feelings
Sun		
Mon		
Tue		

	Events	Feelings
Wed		
Thur		
Fri		
Sat		

Prayer Requests

Here's a place to record prayer requests (either personal ones or ones from your small group). Be sure to record ways you've seen God answer as well.

Date   **Request**   **Praise**

Date   Request   Praise

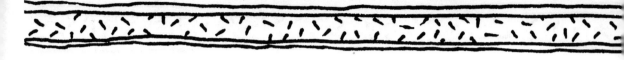